Preparing, Planning and Paying For Long-Term Care: Loopholes for the Middle Class

by Irene Rodway, JD

Publisher's Note

This book is designed to provide information and motivation to our readers. It is sold with the understanding that the publisher is not engaged to render any type of psychological, financial, legal, or any other kind of professional advice. No warranties or guarantees are expressed or implied by the publisher's choice to include any of the content in this volume. No attorney-client or therapeutic relationship is established. Neither the publisher nor the individual author shall be liable for any physical, psychological, emotional, financial, or commercial damages, including, but not limited to, special, incidental, consequential, or other damages. Our views and rights are the same: You are responsible for your own choices, actions, and results.

ISBN: 978-0-9861485-0-7

Summary: Practical advice on how to pay for the long-term care of a loved one.

© 2015 by Irene Rodway, JD

Efforts have been made to gain permission to use the late Owen Darnell's A Room without Doors *Ormond Beach, FL: Flagler Chapter Alzheimer's Association, 1995. Please contact us at the address below if you have rights to this poem.* No copywrite infringement is intended.

All rights reserved. No part of this publication may be reproduced, distributed, or transmitted in any form or by any means, including photocopying, recording, or other electronic or mechanical methods, without the prior written permission of the publisher, except in the case of brief quotations embodied in critical reviews and certain other noncommercial uses permitted by copyright law. For permission requests, write to the publisher, addressed:

Train of Thought Press
2275 Huntington Drive, #306
San Marino, CA 91108

Dedication

To the love of my life, my late husband William X. Madden

To my children & grandchildren

And finally to my life long best friend and amazing sister, Jane Powers Benson

Table of Contents

Introduction 7
Disclaimer 9
Who This Book Is For 10
What You'll Learn 12
Chapter 1: The Longevity Bonus — A Double-Edged Sword 13
    Extended Old Age 13
    The "Curse" of the Middle Class 16
Chapter 2: Talking to Your Parents About End of Life Care 18
    How to Talk to Your Parent About All of This 18
    How To Include Your Siblings 21
    How to Include Your Parent's Spouse 23
    Dealing with the re-emergence of old conflict 23
Chapter 3: Asset Protection Planning 25
    Long-term Care Insurance 25
    Reverse Mortgage 26
    Squirreling Away Assets 27
    Spousal Impoverishment 28
Chapter 4: Early phases of elder care 30
    Senior Centers 32
    Adult Day Care (ADC) 33
    Professional In-Home Care 34
Chapter 5: Heart-Breaking Decision — Out of Home Care 38
    Personal Care Homes vs. Assisted Living Facilities 38
    Nursing Homes 39
    The Paperwork 40
Chapter 6: How Hospice Can Help The Middle Class Pay for Care 42
Chapter 7: Medicaid 45
    Becoming eligible for Medicaid 47

Income...47
   Qualified Income Trust (QIT)..47
   Pensions 47
   Beware the Keogh Plan...47
  Assets..48
  Securities, Stocks, and Bonds 50
Chapter 8: VA Benefits 51
  Other Helpful Tips for Veterans...57
  The Affordable Care Act of 2010 aka "Obamacare"........58
Chapter 9: The Importance of Self-Care and Avoiding Burnout.59
  What is Self Care?...60
Chapter 10: Parting Words 62
Glossary of Terms 64
Suggested Reading..81
  Dementia resources: 81
References...83
Product Recommendation 84

Introduction

Dear Friend,

I may not know you personally, but I bet I could guess many things about you and about what you've experienced thus far. Your sorrow. Your fears. Your concerns —both for the person you love so very much and for yourself. The challenges you've encountered, and the challenges that still lie ahead of you. I understand because I've gone through it already. I'm just a few steps ahead of you. The pain and frustration are still fresh as I type these words.

I can't begin to tell you how much I feel for you. What you're dealing with is an impossible situation, made up of equal parts of sadness, stress and disheartening acceptance of the harsh reality of your situation. But before I go any further, let me tell you something very, very important: you're not alone. During my ordeal, I think I would have lost it were it not for the fact that I knew millions of other caregivers who shared the same predicament. They were also up all night, trying to find answers on the Internet, searching for solutions, begging for more time. More resources. Relief. Comfort.

You are not alone, and you are not the first to face this. I hope this knowledge gives you the strength you need to find answers and carry on.

I am Irene Rodway: lawyer, mother, daughter, wife, and sister. But all of those labels were second to that of "caregiver" when my mother (and later my husband) needed end-of-life care. The change took me by surprise, as I think it does most of us. No one asked me if I was willing to transition from my professional life to that of a caregiver; I was sucked into the vortex because I had aging parents and had married an older man, and my love for my family and my wedding vows truly meant "for better or for worse, in sickness and in health."

My journey through the world of end-of-life care had two phases: first caring for my aging parents, and then (with far more impact), caring for my husband of over 40 years — Bill, the love of my life. Bill was considerably older than me and we had many happy years and three children together before the age difference affected me in a significant way. But one day it hit me, like a sucker punch to the gut, the day his age reared its angry head in the form of mental and physical deterioration.

Once the reality of caregiving and ever-mounting expenses set in, the financial and emotional toll that Bill's end-of-life care took almost wiped me out. I had to put up the hardest fight of my life, navigating the maze of expensive options while dealing with my sadness and grief. This is the raw deal that I hope to spare you, dear reader. I hope to make this easier on you. I know I can't take away the pain, and I know I can't lessen the impact of the impending loss. However, I hope to make planning and paying for long-term care easier for you, and in that way, allow you to spend more of your energy caring for yourself. It may sound cliché, but it's true: if you can care for yourself (which includes allowing yourself time to grieve), you will be better prepared to care for the person entrusted to your care.

When I practiced law years ago, my husband used to tell me, "Irene, clients don't come to you because you know the law. They come to you to show them the loopholes." And that is what the elderly middle class is being forced to do. (And it's probably why you bought this book!) You <u>need</u> to find some loopholes.

Of course, you need to make your own choices. This book is not all-encompassing — it's more like a TV guide in that I will outline potential options which I discovered while wandering through the labyrinth. I don't purport to know or address everything about long-term care. I recognize that each situation is unique. However, it is my hope that this book may be a good reference for you — an acceptable place to start when embarking on your journey as an end-of-life caregiver. It is my greatest hope that you might find some help, comfort or knowledge within these pages.

I wish you the best of luck,

Irene

Disclaimer

Although I am a lawyer, nothing that I write in this book should be considered legal advice. I'll remind you of that periodically throughout this publication, but know this from the start: you should always consult your own attorney or financial advisor before proceeding with any recommendations I have provided in these pages.

This book is based entirely on my own experiences and research. It should not be taken as formal legal suggestions on how to manage your own personal or financial affairs.

This is by no means a complete guide. It is a collection of my own personal experiences and thoughts regarding the limited resources available to those charged with the agonizing task of choosing, planning and paying for long-term care. My intention is that this book will raise your awareness of what resources are available and how to navigate a very complex and convoluted system.

This book does not reflect the thoughts or opinions of Train of Thought Press or its agents or employees.

Who This Book Is For

This book is for anyone looking for practical strategies to plan and pay for caring for an elderly loved one. As you will learn, I took care not only of an elderly parent, but also an older husband. I use the term "parent" and "adult child" throughout this book for the sake of clarity.

In an ideal world, you or your parent would have unlimited financial resources that would enable you to seek out the best possible care for your parent. In reality, money complicates everything and closes more doors than it opens, particularly when you don't have it. This book is for people who fear they make too much to qualify for government assistance but also do not want to deplete their parent's entire estate paying for care if there is another way.

Caring for an elderly parent can be one of the most stressful phases in a person's life. Having another human depending on you is draining, regardless of their age. With an aging parent, there are few guaranteed milestones, and comprehensive resources and guidance are harder to come by. Caring for aging parents is not discussed as frequently in polite conversation, adding a sense of isolation to those entering into that phase of their lives.

Rest assured you are not alone. Recent studies indicate that there are over ten million people in the United States caring for aging parents. That is a huge portion of the population, yet there are no periodicals or classes or philosophies dedicated to caring for aging parents as there are for parenting.

Some of the emotional challenges you're likely to face include anger, sadness, grief, depression, changes in the balance of your intimate relationships, financial changes, feelings of isolation, and questioning or strengthening of faith. Other challenges may include grieving the end of your childhood, strained relationships with siblings and other family members, medical red tape, and legal difficulties.

Unlike children who usually follow a predictable gestation and developmental pattern, aging parents do not develop or progress predictably. This can be disarming and frightening, particularly when health problems, safety concerns, or dementia dominate the experience of caring for your parent. Know that you are not alone in your struggle.

What You'll Learn

This book will cover many important topics related to caring for an aging parent: how to have challenging conversations about your parent's care, asset protection planning, determining what level of care your parent needs, managing your parent's finances, including siblings and spouses in your parent's care team, and qualifying for various government programs. Last but not least, a chapter on how to care for yourself to avoid burnout. Also included is a list of recommendations for further reading.

Chapter 1: The Longevity Bonus — A Double-Edged Sword

It's true: we live longer these days. When you're middle-aged, that sounds wonderful. You can blow out the candles on your 40th birthday and think, "I'm only halfway to the finish line! Maybe not even there yet!"

However, the phenomena of extended old age comes with a truckload of baggage that isn't celebrated in the commercials for Viagra and the like. All of those commercials are cleverly constructed to lead you to believe that you will live healthy and ailment free until the day you die in your sleep, happy as a clam at age 90.

The truth is most of us will experience a slow decline in mental and physical health as we age, prolonged by the many medical advancements we so heartily celebrate. This extended state of living with increasingly significant medical conditions takes a toll on everyone around us, as we struggle to find financial solutions, asset protection planning and affordable assistance with care. The problem is difficult for everyone, in every social class, but it is especially rough on the middle class, who quickly find themselves up against a wall financially, with nowhere to turn.

Extended Old Age

Entering into the Medicare age (65) has traditionally been regarded the same as going into retirement, which used to involve, a long time ago, contemplations of happy ideas such as fantasies of traveling to new places and spending more time with family members. Nowadays though, it is an ever-lengthening stage of life. The expectation that "I could live to 95 or longer" has transformed the idea of retirement into a prospect loaded with apprehension and concern.

When you only expect to live into your seventies, the rest of your life is relatively easy to plan for. You have a few savings which, when combined with a pension and whatever benefits the government offers, may be more than adequate.

However, with the modern medically-induced "fad" of longer life hovering over all couples in their 50's, 60's, and 70's (which some might call a "bonus"), the idea of "relaxing" into retirement after a life of hard work is no longer the reality. Dr. Ken Dychtwald, a gerontologist and public speaker, does not sugarcoat the severity of the problem that accompanies living longer. In a recent Huffington Post article, he said, "...for [many], this 'longevity bonus' will be fraught with pain and suffering. Large numbers of tomorrow's elders could wind up impoverished, left stranded by an absence of financial preparedness and dwindling old age entitlements." (Dychtwald, 2010)

Is it just me, or do you also think he was being sarcastic when he placed quotation marks around the phrase "longevity bonus"?

At any rate, thank you, Dr. Ken Dychtwald, for that is the message I have wanted to communicate for some time now. His statement goes to the heart of my story: how can anyone afford to pay for an older person's care?

And as if we don't have enough problems with the expanded lifespan factor, there is another culprit that hides behind old age — chronic disease. The Center for Disease Control (CDC) has a pleasant demographic for us: at least half of the US population has one or more chronic diseases, and the ratio increases to three out of four if you're 65 or older. It doesn't sound so awful at first, when mentioned in those clinical terms, right? But chronic diseases are expensive, debilitating, and, although sometimes temporarily manageable, often result in death. (CDC, 2015)

Chapter 1: The Longevity Bonus — A Double-Edged Sword

Naturally, there is a distinction between mental and physical aliments, and the complex healthcare, financial and government systems do nothing to ease the transition from good to poor mental health. If a person is declining in health physically, there are a host of different options offered, but patients don't receive the same range of care options if they suffer from Alzheimer's disease or overall mental deterioration. Oftentimes, benefits and solutions will depend greatly on how the aging person is suffering physically, which obviously does nothing to ease the toll on the caretaker or loved ones of someone who suffers from mental illness. As of the writing of this book, there are no government programs that will defray the cost of long-term care for a loved one who has mental issues but no physical limitations.

Susannah Fox, Associate Director of the Pew Research Center's Internet and American Life Project and the study's lead author said, "As more people are able to be saved by medical advances, their lives are being extended, but they're also being sent home medically fragile." She goes on to say that, "[with] fewer or depleted savings, many people are less able to hire non–family help."

In other words, because of increasingly diminished financial resources, more and more healthcare is happening at home. Other options, once far more feasible, have moved out of reach. This longevity bonus (I've come to think of it as a "curse," even though I don't want to be insensitive to those who still view it as a benefit — I've become jaded by my experiences, which I think is understandable) is fraught with an endless array of worries. This is particularly true if, like me, you deeply love the person in your charge.

These additional years of living come with an endless stream of unforeseen health and life issues, all of the savings-depleting kind. You really have to be caring for an older person to realize how quickly these expenditures pile up, with something new cropping up almost on a daily basis. The money you thought would easily carry you through retirement is eaten up by a care system with a voracious and insatiable appetite.

The "Curse" of the Middle Class

Now that you have some perspective on the "longevity bonus" and medically induced extended old age, you're equipped to understand the curse that now plagues the aging middle class. The problem with aging in the middle class these days breaks down into two main issues. The first is that, in your young and productive life, you likely saved for retirement. I'm sure you've saved and saved, envisioning comfortable final days and maybe even something to leave behind for your children or loved ones. However, when chronic diseases start to hit and the longevity "bonus" that modern medicine has provided makes it such that people live far longer than anticipated with many more ailments than anyone ever anticipated, most middle class savings become inadequate. Why? Because health care costs are exorbitant, and retirement savings are finite. Many middle class citizens simply can't afford to pay for the care required during those last years.

The second issue is that the government programs once available to aging citizens are rapidly disappearing in light of the multitudes of seniors requiring the assistance of these programs today. Veteran's benefits are dwindling and are immensely complex to apply for and ultimately receive. Your hard work and existing assets disqualify you from many poverty-assistance programs (even though those assets will do nothing to keep you solvent while paying for incredibly expensive aging healthcare). The healthcare services and hospice care have been commercialized and inflated to the point where it is impossible to afford long-term if you are in the middle class.

At the end of the day, the middle class is left in a confusing and financially disappointing hole. So what is there to do?

You may have heard from friends, co-workers or extended family members about how to begin your long-term care journey financially. They may be telling you to **start protecting assets now** or taking steps early in order to later **qualify for various programs and benefits**. You may also already have a cursory knowledge of placement options for your loved one. But the crux of this matter is that there are financial considerations to keep in mind from the get-go with each and every care option.

Asset protection planning, whether in the context of using Veterans Administration ("the VA") benefits or Medicaid for long-term care, is critically important before moving forward with a particular strategy. You need to ensure that you have been educated as to all the legal planning options you have and how the course you follow impacts other benefits programs. Why? Because the choices you make (even some that do not appear to be related to paying for long-term care) will affect your options, and you need to figure out which choices will open the most (and/or best) options possible.

Reminder: Only attorneys can discuss the law with you, and only attorneys can prepare legal documents for you. Please do not consider these words legal advice. I am simply sharing my experiences in dealing with these matters.

Chapter 2: Talking to Your Parents About End of Life Care

Unlike small children, elders do not have the same medical and supervision needs at various stages. This is what makes caring for aging parents so difficult. Some elders may need hospital care for some time but then be able to return to a lower level of care after certain health concerns are resolved or managed more effectively. The fact that there isn't a predictable progression of care for most elders only adds to the confusion and stress of overseeing a parent's care. This also brings confusion about how involved adult children need to be in ensuring their parent receives the appropriate level of care. Most children want to respect their parent's autonomy and medical privacy for as long as possible. But at a certain point, it becomes clear that adult children need to be involved.

How to Talk to Your Parent About All of This

Often the most difficult part of caring for an aging parent is discussing their care with them directly. Parent-child relationships are complex, and shifts in power dynamic are stressful and confusing. The teenage years are daunting for many parents because children become capable of doing many things for themselves and often "try on" their newfound independence in questionable or unorthodox ways. The parent can no longer dictate their daily activities as they would a younger child. This shift in power is difficult to navigate, causing much tension between parents and children. So too is the shift from a parent-child relationship of healthy adults to a parent-child relationship of healthy adult and dependent elder. Many people resist these natural changes in power, making the transition more difficult. Depending on your parent's cognitive abilities, they may downplay their care needs for your benefit, feel guilty for being a burden, become angry, or outright deny that they need any type of care whatsoever. All these things are normal and part of a difficult emotional transition.

If you feel your parent is resistant to initial conversations about their care or may become angry with you for broaching the subject, you may need to be strategic in how you approach the conversation. Some people have success by presenting issues of elder care from the perspective of personal consideration:

"[Husband] and I were talking about our wills the other day and our long-term plan for our lives and the kids. We decided to draw up a living will and include preferences about our care in the future so that there's as little confusion and stress as possible. Talking about the future with him made me realize that I don't know what your preferences are or if you having a living will or where you'd like to live when you can't live on your own anymore. Have you thought much about those things?"

This gentler, more considerate approach comes across as responsible and concerned rather than serious and intervention-like. This sets the tone for future conversations and hopefully conveys that you do not plan to make decisions without considering their wishes. Collaboration and compassion go hand-in-hand in the early stages of caring for your parent. On the other end of the spectrum are parents who fixate on the changes in their lives.

Constantly discussing health problems, loss of independence, fear of death, and any other challenges does not bother them at all, but may overwhelm others. Often children with this type of parent feel at a loss for how to respond, or as if it is their responsibility to allay their parent's fears. While finding and providing compassionate and adequate care may fall to you, it is no one's responsibility to manage all the emotions that come with aging. You do not need to fix or counterbalance your parent's emotions. Their emotions and fears are valid and should not be negated or downplayed.

Some techniques and tools for handling your parent's emotions may include learning to be an active listener. Active listening involves hearing and reflecting what your parent is saying without offering suggestions or advice. This technique can feel uncomfortable and off to many people at first, but often feels best to the person expressing their feelings. To many people, feeling heard and cared for feels better than a practical discussion of how they might feel better or something equally dismissive. Listening without intending to fix emotions takes work, but is an invaluable social skill you can apply to many other areas of your life.

Some parents may become angry at you for attempting to talk to them about their care. Your concern for their wellbeing and safety may be misconstrued as you taking away their independence. They may feel you are infantilizing them or otherwise insulting their ability to care for themselves. While stressing that your sole motivation is their safety and comfort may be helpful, oftentimes parents can't hear that over their fears about their own decline and facing death. There is no foolproof way to avoid conflict and anger, but attempting to remain grounded in your concern for your parent's comfort and safety is your best bet.

If you feel you are in a constant battle with your parent over their care, remember that you can do nothing to change their perspective or stance. The only thing you can do is change the way you interact with them. While this is by no means meant to convey that you should back down or ignore your feeling that your parent needs more assistance, you do have power to change your attitude toward the situation. When you feel the struggle is getting too much for you to handle, figuratively set the argument or struggle down for a day or two with the intention of coming back to it when you are calmer and less defensive. Again, you do not need to change your stance. But entering into conversations with a less defensive demeanor may signal to your parent that they don't need to be as aggressive or angry as they are.

Many people have found it helpful to make a plan for what they will do directly after having a delicate conversation with their parent. When anticipating a difficult conversation, having a self-care plan for afterward can make the conversation seem less daunting, even if it's only a trick of the mind. Comprehensive self-care will be discussed in more detail later, but planning to go for a run, pick up your favorite takeout, or call a trusted friend to debrief your conversation is an excellent way to prepare to care for yourself after the fact. It also serves as a reminder that life goes on after a difficult task, and that at some point the task will be over.

To that end, it is normal for adult children serving as caretakers to have conflicting feelings about their parent's eventual death. While losing a parent is a difficult emotional process, caring for a parent can be equally difficult. Some children may feel guilty for wishing that this phase would end, while others may go to extraordinary lengths to deny death is approaching or delay death despite increased suffering on the part of the parent. End-of-life care and psychology is complicated and often taboo in polite conversation, leaving many people feeling scared and alone. There is a list of suggested reading material for people facing mortality – either their own or a loved one's – at the end of this book.

How To Include Your Siblings

Family relationships are complicated, and making group decisions is never easy. Some families have a clear hierarchy that makes decision-making easier; an eldest sibling or sibling closest to your parent may step in and lead the way. If you feel your sibling is taking too much control or not contributing enough, it's important to communicate that.

Relational problems and conflict with siblings is likely to escalate when dealing with the care of an aging parent. Lifelong patterns of miscommunication and long-standing sensitivities become more pronounced when emotions are high. Do your part to minimize the impact these conflicts have on the care your parent receives.

Often women put more pressure on themselves to take responsibility for care of their aging parents than men. There is little reason for this; women work outside the home at almost the same rate men do while also often taking primary responsibility for household maintenance and childrearing. Obviously this is not universal, but a study in 2010 indicated that women lost a significant amount of their anticipated income every year due to caring for aging parents, while men lost very little of their anticipated income due to caring for aging parents. In this modern age, it is time to question assumptions about who should care for the elderly. If you have siblings and feel that assumptions have been made about who will care for your parent based on gender, please consider how that will affect each sibling's quality of life and the quality of the care your parent receives. Men and women are equally capable of nurturing and making good decisions.

If you have siblings you feel you need to "wake up" or call to action, it can be difficult to know how to best do so. You may want to consider the method of communication on which you rely; for some siblings it may be alarming to get an e-mail or text message on such a heavy matter. For others, an unannounced phone call may feel too sudden. However you communicate, try to make it in a way that helps your sibling focus on the matter at hand. Asking to set a phone or lunch date with your sibling might yield better results than texting back and forth during the work day.

One factor that makes including siblings in the decision-making process difficult is distance. If you live closer to your parent, you may be expected to shoulder more of their care than a sibling who lives farther away. Emotional distance has perhaps a greater impact; if your sibling had a strained relationship with your parent or hasn't been on speaking terms for some time, involving them in your parent's care may be more stressful than helpful. If you're unsure of your sibling's willingness to be involved, it's okay to ask. Perhaps they feel comfortable contributing financially, but not in making decisions, or perhaps they have difficulty with medical decisions but not legal decisions. There is no right or wrong way to divide up the giant task of caring for a family member. The important thing is to make an effort to include everyone who might be able to help.

How to Include Your Parent's Spouse

Frequently, one parent begins to need care before the other. If your parent is married – whether to your other parent or not – it is important to consider their spouse's needs when deciding what kind of care your parent needs. While there are many facilities that welcome couples who need different levels of care, some do not. Separating your parent from their spouse can feel punitive and harsh when it could be avoided. If your parent's spouse is able to provide adequate support, a parent who cannot perform all ADLs or IADLs can remain living independently for longer. But it is still important to check in with your parent's spouse about how they are managing; the stress of caring for an aging or ailing spouse might become unmanageable, yet they feel guilty about asking for more assistance or as though they should be able to manage it all. They may feel tremendous relief at even a simple inquiry into how things are going, if it is couched well.

Dealing with the re-emergence of old conflict

It is common for adult children to re-experience things from childhood when caring for their aging parent. It is also common for old resentments and grudges to resurface. If you resented your parent for not allowing you to pursue a certain hobby, or for forcing you to dress a certain way, or for the way they chose to discipline you, feelings will probably arise that make it difficult to provide the loving, compassionate care you feel you should be able to give. Some people try to stuff these feelings down and "leave the past in the past," while others cannot do so and feel the need to rehash old conflicts. This resurgence of grievances may also arise between siblings; the fact that your sister always got new clothes while you got hand-me-downs, or that your brother was allowed to date at a younger age than you were, or that your sister always embarrassed you in front of your friends, might needle its way into discussions about your parent's care. While it can be helpful to acknowledge these feelings, they are usually not conducive to making positive choices and decisions and building effective sibling alliances.

Chapter 3: Asset Protection Planning

I'm not sure where you are at in your journey to plan for, provide, and pay for long-term care. This chapter is for those who are in the first stages, or who are taking proactive steps to prepare for future challenges in the journey. I've presented several strategies regarding early financial actions to take that will lessen your burden later on when you are faced with impending long-term care expenses for a spouse or loved one. I've tried to present both pros and cons for each option.

Long-term Care Insurance

Long-term care insurance is insurance you take out on yourself to ensure against catastrophic expense incurred with the cost of growing old. Like all insurance policies you may end up needing it, or you may never need it. In order for these policies to be affordable, they have to be taken out when you are in your fifties or sixties when the premiums are reasonable. By reasonable I mean $200 to $300 a month. You see the dilemma — you take out insurance that you may or may not need and pay premiums for 20, 30, or even 40 years for a policy you may never need. Make certain the policy has an inflation clause; nursing home care today may be $150 per day, but in ten years it could be $400 per day. You will also want to check to make sure there is no cap on benefits. Extending the time of insurability can also save money. In other words, you could agree that you pay for the first 90 days of care yourself, similar to a deductible on your health or car insurance, in exchange for an extension on the length of time covered and reduced premiums.

The vast majority of people who go into a nursing home are dead within a year. It could be possible that you pay premiums for thirty years and never collect. Many of these insurance companies become insolvent, so do not shop by price alone. It is my experience that you are better off going with a name brand insurance company. You want the policy to be there in the future.

Make certain any long-term care insurance policy provides for care in a personal care home. Many policies just pay if you are moved into a skilled nursing facility. The majority of care in old age is comfort care, not skilled nursing care. Medicaid and the VA will only pay for skilled nursing care, so make certain that your private pay insurance covers personal care homes or services that will allow you to age in your home.

If you do elect to take out long-term care insurance, make sure that Alzheimer's and old age dementia are **specifically covered**. Many policies that do provide for Alzheimer's will not cover for Alzheimer's and old age dementia only —under the terms of the policy, the insured must also have at least two physical disabilities or impairment of daily living, such as incontinence, or the inability to walk, shower, bathe, or feed themselves. Some policies only pay for skilled care facilities. You cannot collect if the insured is living at home or is in an assisted living facility.

Finally, do not take the insurance broker's word for coverage. Obtain a copy of the policy and have it reviewed by an independent lawyer or see several different policies and review all policies with a trusted family member or friend. This is NOT car insurance, and not all policies are the same. However, if you're reading this book, it's likely already too late to take out a long-term care policy. If your loved one already has any type of debilitating illness, you won't be able to get a policy, and even if you can, the premiums will not be affordable. You have to apply for insurance before the serious health problems begin.

Reverse Mortgage

Let's assume you are not rich enough to pay $5,000 to $7,000 a month for nursing home care or a long-term care policy is not an option because you are not insurable and it's not affordable. Some people may advise you to apply for a reverse mortgage (also know as a Home Equity Conversion Mortgage), but you shouldn't — I could write an entire book on why not to go down a reverse mortgage route. The basic problem with a reverse mortgage is that your personal residence is not a countable asset under the Veterans Administration or Medicaid (the two most well-known assistance programs).

Once you put a reverse mortgage on your personal residence, you have converted a non-countable asset into a countable stream of income. Depending on your age and the value of your home, you could get a stream of income large enough to disqualify you from benefits but not enough to pay for the entire cost. Although the reverse mortgage is written as a loan and may not disqualify you from all programs, this seems a poor way to go. I don't recommend a reverse mortgage because you are still responsible for taxes and insurance, and if you pull out income every month, this will disqualify you from Medicaid or VA Benefits.

Squirreling Away Assets

Most people think that giving assets to your children or to your likely beneficiaries is a good way to go about removing assets, but I cannot tell you one way or another. The main things to consider when reallocating your assets are: Is there a record of these assets? What types of records are there of these assets? Who has access to these records? Do these assets show up on your income tax returns? Can a halfway decent, intelligent attorney locate these assets? If yes, you have to assume that Medicaid will figure it out.

Also, ask yourself: are your kids in a stable marriage? By giving these assets to your kids, you make those assets subject to division in a divorce. These are assets that also can be lost in a personal injury lawsuit; these are assets your children have to explain to the various taxing authorities.

You've probably thought, "Maybe I can I give away under $10,000 each year as a gift to avoid inheritance tax?" The answer is yes, but we are not talking about gift taxes here. We are talking about qualifying for Medicaid, which is totally different from being taxed. When my husband was in a nursing home, one of his roommates qualified for Medicaid and several VA benefits because he allegedly suffered from temporary insanity and subsequently depleted all of his assets. He also qualified due to his income, but both benefits depend on assets as well as an income threshold.

LOOPHOLE: Trying to qualify for Medicaid often causes a great deal of stress and makes people to act in ways they would not normally (such as going to Vegas and spending $10,000 to $20,000 at the craps tables, or buying expensive toys which instantly depreciate such as ATVs, motorcycles, etc.). You could also develop an addiction to buying Gucci or Prada purses. These spendthrift ways are often triggered by the stress of taking care of an elderly spouse or parent, which I certainly do not advocate. All of these sudden purchases deplete your assets and put you in a much better position to qualify for Medicaid, but the kicker is that they don't protect you from the five-year look-back period. In some cases that I've seen, this method of asset depletion has been successful, however, you should consult an elder law attorney before making any big financial decisions. And, of course, defrauding Medicaid and/or Medicare is illegal.

Spousal Impoverishment

If the person you are managing long-term care for is your spouse, you are considered the "community spouse." You may be afraid that you will go broke and wind up homeless. An elder law attorney informed me of the Spousal Anti-Impoverishment Act. What this act means is that the healthy spouse (the community spouse) can keep some of the income, an amount that is referred to as the minimum monthly needs allowance. You have to fill out an application provided by the Medicaid caseworker upon which you will claim costs of supporting yourself — monies such as rent, mortgage payments, property taxes, utilities, and insurance. The minimum amount a spouse can keep is 150% of federal poverty levels.

There are also maximum amounts the spouse can keep. This varies by state, but in my case (Georgia) the maximum amount was $2,432. Even if you qualify as far as income goes, you still have to consider assets. There was no break for me — assets in either of our names counted towards my allowance. I had an unlimited spousal obligation. Medicaid makes no exceptions as far as assets are concerned; our asset amount was $118,000 — not nearly enough to support me for another 20 years. There is no allowance for age discrepancy either; whether my remaining lifespan was three years or 23 years made no difference in the qualifying process.

Neither the federal government nor the individual states set the amount each year; it's a fixed amount set by Medicaid. This doesn't seem fair since the cost of living in LA or NYC is much greater than in Hope, Arkansas. This is why many people think about hiding assets. I'll discuss Medicaid and other benefits in greater depth later on, but now I'll describe some placement options for care and how to pay for them.

Chapter 4: Early phases of elder care

It's a given that when a loved one has begun to age and decline in health, the best place for them to be is in their own home — often referred to as "aging in place".

Early phases of elder care usually include brief adult child or home health worker check-ins and assistance with homemaking activities in your parent's own home. This phase of care is considered adequate for elders who have not exhibited major decline in memory and do not have health problems that significantly interfere with their functioning. Relocation to an independent living facility is also considered an early phase of elder care; residents are considered capable of managing their own affairs and seeking medical treatment when necessary.

You might consider moving in with your loved one or having them come to live with you. Resting in a place of comfort and familiarity is far preferable to spending the end of one's precious life in a cold, sterile facility. For as long as possible, keeping your loved one safe in your own care is usually by far the most preferable option.

Once you've made the decision to care for your loved one as they age, you will most likely feel like it's your duty to take care of them on your own. This is a fallacy, and you shouldn't let yourself get caught in this trap. *You will need help, and getting it set up sooner rather than later is key.*

No one is really prepared for the daily grind of in-home healthcare. If you try to do it on your own, you risk ending up exhausted, irritable and incapable of continuing to care for your loved one. You need to have help and support from paid, in-home healthcare providers. If you do not get qualified in-home assistance, then you could succumb to one of several negative scenarios, such as: you age and begin to get sick as well; any spare moment your family has is spent giving you a break; family members may become resentful of the disruption in their lives and could take it out on you. Life gets hard, and then it gets harder.

The end of a loved one's life can be a special and cathartic time for you and your family. It's an awful shame to squander that fleeting experience by thinking you can care for someone all by yourself and subsequently becoming frustrated and upset instead of enabling everyone to enjoy the time that's left with your loved one. This is where professional caregivers can relieve you of some of that burden and truly help you cherish the end-of-life journey.

Within all of that, there are many things to consider when caring for an aging person in your home. The first and most important consideration, which will determine what the rest of your options are, is whether or not your loved one is capable of performing the activities of daily living (hereafter referred to as "ADL").

These activities are exactly what you might expect them to be. They include:

- Basic toiletry functions (teeth brushing, bathing, and using the toilet)

- Essential culinary activities (feeding oneself, cooking basic meals)

- Necessary motor skills (moving from a bed to a chair, dressing oneself)

If all of these skills can still be performed, loneliness and isolation become the main issue for aging seniors. If this is the case, a quality option is finding and enrolling your loved one in a local senior center program or an adult day care. These programs provide daily supervision so the caregiver can still work and manage a household, but the loved one can still live at home and sleep in their own bed.

Senior Centers

Most cities these days have senior centers, a type of community center where the elderly can spend time during the day interacting with others and engaging in various activities. The best way to find these civically funded programs is to contact your local senior resource service or your community recreation office and find a center near you. Many centers also have sites online and can quickly be found with a simple Google search. Once you find a center (or several) near you, it's best to take a tour with your loved one to see if it's a place where they'll be comfortable and happy spending their days.

These programs generally run weekdays and are very inexpensive — they're funded by your municipality and sometimes even by the state or federal government. That being the case, it may only cost you several dollars a day for lunch or snacks. Activities are varied and, depending on the facility, may include exercise options, games, dancing, crafting, and reading. Some centers in larger cities may contract daily events such as guest speakers or entertainers, and some even provide transportation to and from your home.

Though senior centers are a nice place for your loved one to socialize with others, no one will look after them per se. There are generally staff members who can perform CPR but they don't pay trained medical personnel. Centers won't administer medication or remind your loved one to take their meds. They'll provide meals, but they don't take into account any dietary restrictions like allergies or diabetes. Basically, these centers are spaces where seniors can spend time during their days with others — they are not care facilities.

If you decide to take your loved one to spend time in the center, it can be helpful to develop relationships with other residents. When I started taking my husband, Bill, to our local center, I found a veteran sitting nearby (they'll usually wear hats with their military affiliation). I told him Bill was also a vet and asked if he could sit with them for the day. He wouldn't accept money, but I'd bring cigarettes and pizza or offer to pay for their lunches. When my mother was there, we brought her knitting needles and yarn. Although by then her eyesight was poor and she was unable to read patterns, her knitting hobby was a real icebreaker that resulted in socialization. Making friends and enlisting other residents to help keep an eye on your loved one is a valuable experience for everyone — this is the start of the rainy day for which we've all been saving, so spread as much sunshine as you can.

The biggest caveat in all of this is, of course, your senior's capabilities to perform ADL; most importantly, **senior centers will not admit anyone who is incontinent**. If your loved one has reached this stage, it is time to consider other options.

Adult Day Care (ADC)

Adult day cares were formed primarily as a method for the aging American population to have a better transition from health to end-of-life care. There are more than 5,000 of these centers in the country today, and that number is growing. Some are independently owned and operated; others are members of a chain. Sarah Care is one of the conglomerates that provide adult day cares nationwide; however, they do franchise out some locations, so always be prepared to tour and interview before you decide where to enroll your loved one.

Adult day cares are similar to senior centers save for a few details: they are open for more hours (usually 10 – 14 a day), they retain nurses and certified nursing assistants (CNAs) on staff, and they cost money. Out of pocket payment for ADC centers generally runs anywhere from 50 to 75 dollars a day that, sadly, is not covered by any government-provided programs (VA, Medicaid etc.). However, when enrolling your loved one in an ADC, speak with the director of the center and tell them you will need financial assistance. Programs are constantly changing; while some are defunded, others suddenly appear and the operators will always know the best options at the time.

LOOPHOLE: For instance, I was fortunate in stumbling upon a relatively unknown VA program while my husband's health was declining. Since he was already qualified and in the system, we were quickly enrolled in a program called Contract Adult Day Healthcare. This program was implemented to enable veterans in ailing health to remain at home for as long as possible when they might otherwise require institutional care, such as an assisted living facility or a nursing home. It was beneficial because it wasn't dependent on any service-connected disabilities or related to income or assets. Always discuss potential options with the admissions director; they may have information you might not find otherwise.

Aside from cost, a big consideration when choosing between an ADC and a senior center is your loved one's medical condition. If your loved one has deteriorated mentally (Alzheimer's, dementia and the like) it's best to choose an ADC — they are secure facilities that retain staff able to supervise your loved one safely. Similarly, if a senior requires any sort of ongoing medical treatment, or takes pills, the nurses on staff can manage those care needs. ADCs also are capable of performing rehabilitation services for a loved one after a hospital stay. Additionally, ADCs are willing to admit people with incontinence issues.

The Commission on Accreditation of Rehabilitation Facilities (CARF) is the non-profit independent entity that accredits ADCs.

Professional In-Home Care

When your loved one can no longer easily perform the activities of daily living but is not yet ready to move into residential care, it's time to consider getting in-home help.

Being the full-time caregiver for someone you love quickly becomes mentally and emotionally exhausting. This loved one who was once a whole, vital person now depends on you to complete actions as simple as going to the bathroom and cleaning him or herself. It's painful and scary — not to mention exhausting — to watch this deterioration of a person who once was so capable. No one should have to do it alone.

Help from family members might be an option, but these days many families have splintered across the country. Siblings have their own lives; children have their own families. Enlisting their help can become complicated and emotionally draining.

By far the best option is to hire a skilled professional to work with you in your home. In-home caregivers are broken up into two categories — they're either independently employed or employed through a service. If you choose to hire independently, you should always run a background check, call as many references as possible, and utilize an independent contractor agreement (available on LegalZoom.com) before allowing someone to care for your loved one. These measures will ensure reliable and safe care.

There are several types of professionals available for this role — certified nursing assistants, home health aides, and personal care assistants are all options, depending on your unique situation. It is important to communicate regularly with your parent's home health worker if they have one, as they are usually well-versed in elder needs and what levels of care are appropriate.

Certified nursing assistants (CNA) are trained, registered, and licensed medical professionals who can tend to the comfort and medical needs of your loved one. They can monitor vital signs, tend to wounds or physical conditions, and help your loved one with their activities of daily living.

As independent contractors, most CNAs make between $11 and $15 an hour, depending on your local rates. If they are contracted through a service or agency, you'll pay a lot more

($22 to $27 an hour) but you'll have the security of a service supporting you — if your CNA ever falls ill or takes personal time, the service will send someone else so you aren't suddenly left without assistance. The other benefit of hiring through a service is that payment agreements, background checks, and thorough screening have all been completed before the CNA ever reaches you.

Home health aides (HHA) are people who have chosen a career that many don't because they have a passion for caring for others. They can be hired, again, independently or through a service and care for your loved one's ADL. Though they don't have formal medical training, they typically have enough experience to be competent in case of an emergency (CPR certified and the like). They spend time with your loved one, providing companionship and mental stimulation as opposed to merely providing ADL support. Pricing for these services vary, typically $10 to $13 an hour if they're independently hired and $22 to 27 an hour, depending on the service. Usually HHAs will also cook and do light housekeeping.

Personal care assistants (PCA) usually perform in-home chores that your loved one can no longer complete on their own. Shopping, cooking, and cleaning are typical PCA duties, but they will also provide companionship and supervision. These professionals can assist your loved one with basic ADL, but typically you would hire a home health aide or a CNA if incontinence were a consideration. Hiring a PCA independently is the best option — it can be hard to find a service that exclusively hosts these professionals. Even if you do find one, you'll be paying a lot more if you go through a service. If you hire someone on your own, be sure to check references and conduct a background check.

There are government funds available for skilled nursing care but very few funds for help with activities of daily living (ADL). This includes bathing, changing of clothes, feeding yourself, drinking by yourself, going to the bathroom, brushing teeth, etc. I call this custodial care. Your loved one is not able to stay by themselves, yet is not so badly off that he or she needs skilled nursing home care and around-the-clock nursing care.

Lack of funding for personal care assistance seems foolish and short sighted. Many people are residents of nursing homes in skilled nursing facilities who could very well stay at home with a caregiver or live at a personal care home for thousands of dollars less but do not because these placement options do not qualify for government assistance. There are government programs that help you defray the costs.

So how do I find an independent care worker?

First, ask around. If someone is currently or has recently cared for a loved one, they may be able to point you in the right direction. Many people who work at existing nursing homes are not paid very well and may be looking for additional work. Sometimes these people might have transportation issues, but generally these can be worked around. You should offer three to four dollars an hour more than these workers currently make and you'll likely have a steady stream of applicants.

There are many people out there willing and able to help you with your aging-in-place journey; you just have to make sure you find the right solution for your loved one and for your bank account. Sadly, government or VA programs do not wholly fund many of these options. However, it never hurts to check. You may be eligible for a percentage of assistance depending on your situation. The social worker is the gatekeeper for many of these resources. As in life some social workers know more than others. That is why it is important to educate yourself.

Chapter 5: Heart-Breaking Decision — Out of Home Care

Once you've exhausted your options for in-home care, it's time to consider other strategies to keep your loved one comfortable somewhere else. In this chapter I'll discuss external options for care, such as personal care homes, assisted living facilities, nursing homes, and, finally, hospice care.

Personal Care Homes vs. Assisted Living Facilities

Personal care homes are group homes, often small, taking two or three guests, whereas assisted living facilities are typically larger. Many homes allow husbands and wives to live together. The kicker is that most of these expensive care facilities are private pay only. The majority of aging seniors just need custodial care, but there are no government programs that help pay for these costs. Personal care homes and assisted living facilities both become very expensive, very quickly. It's important to explore all your options for paying for these wildly expensive end-of-life care solutions before you make any commitments.

You have to pay for personal care homes and/or assisted living facilities yourself unless you have long-term care insurance. I've discussed the pros and cons of these policies already, but always take care to deeply explore your financial options before you commit to a particular strategy.

IMPORTANT TIP:

The Veterans Administration has an "Aide and Attendance" program, also known as "improved pension benefits." This program will pay a certain amount towards these external placement options. (As of writing this book, the amount was $1,700 per month.) Often the process of applying for Aide and Attendance can take over a year. However, if your loved one is approved, the government will make the benefits retroactive to the date you first applied. Aide and Attendance is also available for the widow of a veteran. I will discuss VA programs in depth in another chapter.

LOOPHOLE: Medicare will pay for a rehabilitation facility but not for custodial care (such as personal care homes or assisted living). You might be able to discuss options with your loved one's primary care physician in order to qualify them for admittance into a facility. Sometimes the doctor can write a statement emphasizing the loved one's inability to perform the activities of daily living (ADL) to such an extent that it's labeled a "physical disability," which then becomes relevant to Medicare.

Nursing Homes

So now we are left with skilled nursing homes. It's a difficult decision to put a loved one in a home, but sometimes it just has to be done. Please do not extend a promise to a loved one saying "I will never, ever, ever put you in a nursing home." It is a promise that is almost impossible to keep. You may think the biggest decision is "Where do I put my loved one when I finally make the decision that I can no longer take care of them all by myself?"

Yes, that is a big decision. It rips your heart out and you feel like a failure. You promised your mother/father/sister/spouse that you would never put them in a home, and here you are doing it. Then when you make that terrible decision, you find out that assisted living costs around $2,000 to $3,000 a month and a nursing home costs $5,000 to $7,000 a month and climbing — and to what end?

Something that frustrates me is the fact that the government is not even discussing how to pay for long-term end of life care or nursing homes. It's not considered an important enough issue to get attention. Instead, our country is consumed with issues such as who can marry whom and what people can or can't do with their own bodies while an entire portion of the population — the elderly middle class — is sinking into poverty and substandard care. The issue here is that no middle class family can afford this type of care for any sustained length of time.

So… your loved one's condition is not getting better; you are just making them comfortable and easing their pain. The quality of life isn't improving and often the only visitor they have is you. Most family and friends cannot visit depressing nursing homes for any extended period of time. It's important that you not feel guilty if you can no longer provide care around the clock.

Prolonging your loved one's life eats up all of the financial resources. You do not want your loved one to die, but on the other hand, every day they live costs big money.

You simply have to get your loved one qualified for some sort of assistance, whether you're looking at Medicaid, Medicare, or the VA. Most of these programs are dependent on assets and income, even though you likely can't handle these expenses on your own, even with your existing finances. They look at your parents' income and assets, not yours. You have no legal obligation to pay for end of life care for your parents. You do have an obligation to a spouse. I was given advice to divorce my husband so that I would have no legal obligation. Some couples have to do this. I just couldn't, even if it meant that I had to live under a bridge.

But if you've made the decision to admit your loved one to a home before securing the finances (which can happen), you must know how to fill out the paperwork so you don't end up bankrupt and living under a bridge down the road.

The Paperwork

When you are at the admissions office at the nursing home you will be handed a stack, probably six inches thick, of forms, information packets, and more forms. **Be very careful before you sign anything.** Make sure you understand what everything means and how it implicates you or affects your eligibility for benefits and services.

LOOPHOLE: Most homes have a financial responsibility sheet. This allegedly asks what entity is paying for the patient's care. Hidden in the small print will be a sentence or two that states, "You personally sign as being responsible." That means if your parents' funds run out or any type of government funding is cut during their stay, then you are responsible. Do not sign this as an individual. Instead, sign the POWER OF ATTORNEY line so that you are in no way personally responsible for any debts.

The home cannot refuse to accept the resident based solely upon your personal refusal to become personally obligated. If the patient is your sibling or grandparent or friend, the loved one cannot be refused admission to the home just because you (a third party) aren't willing to be held responsible for the finances; in fact, it is a state and federal offense to deny admission for this reason alone. However, this issue becomes trickier when the loved one is a spouse.

If the loved one is a spouse, my personal advice is the same — do not sign yourself up to be personally responsible. Use the power of attorney and admit doing so. My advice is to pay an attorney to prepare these documents and/or use a legal document preparation website (e.g. LegalZoom.com or RocketLawyer.com).

Chapter 6: How Hospice Can Help The Middle Class Pay for Care

The biggest myth is that Hospice is just for the final days and hours of life. This is NOT TRUE. Hospice care programs exist to provide *comfort* to the loved one and family but *not to cure*. If you and your loved one have made the decision to not further any medicinal means to attempt a cure, e.g. hospital admission, surgery, chemo, or radiation, your loved one may qualify. If your aim is merely comfort or to provide palliative care rather than a cure, hospice may be an appropriate placement. Not everyone is accepted into hospice programs, but they can be beneficial.

GIANT LOOPHOLE:

Hospice care is not designed to be a free nursing home, but it *can be*.

If your loved one has old age dementia or Alzheimer's with no other acute or life limiting physical disability, he or she will not qualify for hospice care. However, if you can find (in addition to dementia or Alzheimer's) any life-limiting physical condition such as vascular disease, cancer, failure to thrive, Parkinson's, etc. your loved one will most likely qualify.

Medicare and VA pay for hospice care. If your loved one has a Medicare condition, or conditions that will limit life expectancy, call a hospice service and inquire as to whether or not your loved one qualifies. All hospice groups are for profit and some are more aggressive in marketing than others. In other words, shop around for a hospice program that will work with you.

Once the hospice program has accepted your loved one, s/he will qualify for many benefits such as: aides to do light housekeeping, prepare meals, bathing, grooming, etc. You may also get to engage with a social worker, receive health monitoring services provided by an R.N., have medications distributed, and even

Chapter 6: How Hospice Can Help The Middle Class Pay for Care

receive respite care (for the caregiver) for four to five days a month (if your loved one stays home).

Medicare will also pay for out of home hospice — neither your assets nor income are a criteria. This is a little known loophole for the middle class. The only consideration is health. Once accepted into hospice, it's very difficult to get kicked out. Hospice is a for-profit company and it is in the company's best interest to keep people in. Remember, Medicare pays for healthcare and Medicaid provides aid for the poor. Under Medicaid, income and assets are considered. Under Medicare the only criteria is health. I knew one individual who was in hospice for four years.

The Veterans Administration criteria for hospice are much more stringent. The VA will generally pay for 90 days of inpatient care. After the initial admission, the VA doctor has to re-certify eligibility every 90 days. However, the VA will pay for nursing home placement for a qualified hospice. If your loved one is sick enough that you're considering a nursing home, you may instead want to consider getting qualified for hospice care. Tell your primary care physician that your loved one is getting off all medications and wants to be reassigned to geriatrics and/or a palliative care unit. It has been my experience that the sooner you get your loved one to these units, the sooner you will get the care you need. The VA is more likely to provide transportation for those types of medical visits. Again, these services are not dependent on any type of service connected disability. For hospice, there is also no income or asset consideration.

Hospice care can also be provided in-home. It will generally include an aide visiting your loved one's home at predetermined times, four or five days a week, giving you a break from your care duties. Sometimes the service isn't quite so reliable with their scheduling (in my experience), but they are trained professionals who can deal with medical things that you often can't. These aides will take vital signs and help your loved one take a bath or shower, which is a huge blessing. When my husband was sick, he was very reluctant to allow me to manage his personal hygiene. At one point he went three weeks without showering properly — you can imagine the smell. He did allow the hospice worker to help him bathe, as she was trained and could keep him safe.

The VA can also help with expenses for at-home services through a program called "improved benefits," or **Aide and Attendance**. Aide and Attendance is dependent on income, assets, and the marital status of the veteran. However, you can deduct medical expenses when reporting these numbers to the VA — medical expenses include medications, household help, doctors' visits, and anything covered by Medicare part A and B. VA benefits do not have a look-back period, as with Medicaid, which always has a five-year look-back period. This means that you can transfer assets out of your name the day before applying for VA benefits and still qualify. But you cannot do that for Medicaid. Also note that Medicaid does not pay for hospice — but Medicare does, the rationale being that funding aides and caregivers is far less expensive than paying for complex operations, radiation, or other medicines. In the following two chapters, I will expand on Medicaid and VA Benefits.

Chapter 7: Medicaid

Medicaid has, by default, become the long-term care insurance of the middle class. Neither our state legislatures nor Congress are even addressing the public policy issues of how we as a society should pay for long-term care of our seniors so we have a makeshift system of private insurance, family caregivers, and Medicaid (as a last resort).

I'm guessing that you are part of the great middle class or have modest wealth. You want to provide your loved one with quality long-term care without impoverishment (meaning financial destitution). In my case, I did not want to live in a cardboard box or under a bridge. We have to apply for and qualify for government benefits, either Medicaid or veteran's benefits. There is no other choice but to turn to a government program.

Federal and state governments share Medicaid expenses. At the federal level, anyone who qualifies for Medicaid gets covered. The states also decide who gets covered. The individual states have the discretion on how far they expand Medicaid to serve under-insured populations. Fewer resources can mean narrower coverage on a state-by-state basis. In other words, if you live in Georgia, but your loved one lives in Maine, it is the Maine state government that qualifies your loved one for Medicaid if s/he stays in Maine. If you were planning to transfer your loved one to your place of domicile, then Georgia would dictate the qualifications and guidelines. Most states have the same income and assets cap, but they can and do change. You need to call your local Medicaid office to check these amounts.

In order to qualify, you need to "impoverish" the loved one, and, if you are a couple, impoverish yourself. There is a program called the Spousal Impoverishment Act, which I described earlier, that allows the non-inpatient spouse to protect a certain amount of assets and monthly income. This program is okay if the non-resident spouse is older or close in age to the spouse. In my case the Spousal Impoverishment Act was not useful.

Keeping $119,000 in assets didn't really help since I will hopefully live for a long time, so I then sought out elder law attorneys who without exception wanted to charge $7,000 to $10,000 to establish elaborate trusts (which sometimes don't work). The fee charged also covers a hearing before Medicaid. The hearing will be necessary because Medicaid will often initially deny a claim.

So let's discuss Medicaid. There is a huge difference between Medicaid and Medicare. Medicare does not pay for long-term care. That's right —Medicare DOES NOT PAY! It's unfortunate that Medicaid and Medicare have such similar names. I myself have mistakenly said one name while meaning the other. Both programs are called entitlement programs and they tend to benefit the older and sicker population. The verbal mistake of interchanging the names Medicaid and Medicare is often not caught and corrected. This can have really tragic consequences. People hear that Medicare pays for extended nursing home care and they know they qualify for Medicare so what's the worry? **Medicare does not pay for extended nursing home care!** (I keep it straight to myself by remembering that Medi*care "cares"* for sick and disabled people, whereas Medi*aid "aids"* poor people). Medicare is automatic once you turn 65 but to qualify for Medicaid you must meet certain income and asset requirements.

If your loved one is injured and is in the hospital for five days or more, they can be transferred directly from the hospital to a rehabilitation facility, usually a nursing home (which is what happened to my mother). She had a small stroke and could no longer take care of herself. Medicare only pays for 80 percent of the daily room rate. You need to pay for the 20 percent not covered. Some insurance plans cover the 20 percent deficit for 100 days. But when Medicare runs out... WHAT DO YOU DO?

CHAPTER 7: MEDICAID

Becoming eligible for Medicaid

So how do you get Medicaid to pay for your loved one? You help them become eligible. Eligibility for Medicaid depends on two factors: income and assets.

Income

Qualified Income Trust (QIT)

A Qualified Income Trust (QIT) is sometimes referred to as a Miller Trust. Many families who have severely disabled children and need government assistance use the QIT.

Medicaid prohibits attorneys and eligibility specialists such as caseworkers who work for the state from advising anyone to take specific actions to make them eligible. This would be practicing law without a license. I am of the opinion that the state does not want you to know what your rights are. There are different rules for income and assets for veteran's benefits, which will be addressed in the section on veteran's benefits.

Pensions

Pensions generate income and are generally not countable as an asset. Pensions are countable as an asset only to the extent that you or your loved one has the right to draw the money in a lump sum. If you don't have the right to draw the money in a lump sum because it is under the right and control of your employer, the monthly income is countable as income but the actual corpus you have is not countable as an asset.

Beware the Keogh Plan

Your employer also operates your Keogh plan but it is considered different from a pension because, under most Keogh plans, you can take a lump sum of money out of it. Yes, you incur taxes and a penalty if you do so, but since the money is technically under your control, it's considered a countable asset and can disqualify you from Medicaid. I call this the double whammy in that the monthly distribution is countable as income and the corpus is counted as an asset. You have a similar double whammy problem (countable as income and assets) with your IRA.

Many elder law attorneys will tell you that the IRA problem can be fixed by purchasing an annuity; usually this is true since once an annuity starts making distributions, you have no say-so about it. Definitely consult with an elder law attorney before going down this route. Don't trust your friendly local insurance broker. Annuities have a huge upfront cost where five to six percent is taken at the front end and you have to live with the annuity payments for the rest of your life. Annuities can also trigger income tax issues and estate issues. You should read your annuity policy very carefully to see whether and to what extent the policy can be cashed out. An annuity is a countable asset for Medicaid only to the extent that you can remove the funds in a lump sum.

Assets

As I said before, qualifying involves income as well as assets, so let's discuss assets!

In discussing assets for the purpose of Medicaid, the big item to look out for is the five-year look-back period. This means that Medicaid can look over all your financial records, your stock accounts, your bank records, and credit card bills, and will disallow coverage for a certain number of months if you have transferred assets or cash without fair value. They consider that the sole purpose of doing this is to get your assets lower so that you will qualify for Medicaid. The state looks for actual transfers (i.e. you write out a check to your grandchild for $1,000). This may disqualify you from benefits if the caseworker feels this $1,000 was for the purpose of depleting assets. However, you could write out a check for $1,000 a month and say it was for custodial care and you will probably get away with it.

Examples:

I give $2,000 each to my five children for a total of $10,000. I give it to them for a birthday present and Christmas present. This will disqualify you from Medicaid. If you do things that way for a certain period of time, you will be kicked out of the system or never get in at all. However, if the $10,000 is used for airfare and hotel rooms to visit your dying loved one, there is a purpose other than transferring assets, namely to give care and peace and comfort to the loved one. Paying for the airfare, hotel, etc. is better than paying the money to your family directly.

If you take the same $10,000 and blow it on a cruise, it may have the consequence of transferring $10,000 out of your estate but the main reason was not to thwart Medicaid.

You sell your house in which you presently live, or you sell your house and your second home, bundle the money together and buy a new residence. You take all that cash money out of your asset pool and put it into a family home, which is an exempt asset. The key point to note is that whatever the asset transfer is that has been completed in the prior five years, that asset transfer must have another purpose other than transferring assets to thwart Medicaid.

So, if you own a home, now is the time to put in new windows and a sun porch, a second bedroom, the in-law suite or a new roof. This will generally not disqualify you from Medicaid. You may have other assets in resources such as social security, pensions, rental income, or stocks. These are all considered assets even though they produce income.

Securities, Stocks, and Bonds

As I use the word 'securities' in this book, it means stocks, bonds (including government bonds), treasury bills, stock options, future contracts, IOUs, mutual funds, money market funds, and any other financial instrument of any kind, including trustees. If you have sold your home and taken back a security deed or trust deed, this is considered an asset as well as monthly income. There is some hope with securities that Medicaid does not presume to belong entirely to the applicant or his/her spouse. The security is presumed to belong to the person whose name is on the certificate.

A different percentage can be accepted if the applicant can prove that the securities actually belong to someone else. Securities that are publicly traded are valued at the most recently traded price on the stock market, not the price at which you bought them. Sometimes a situation can occur with family-owned businesses that have been incorporated. Some securities can't be traded or are difficult to trade and you may be able to make a case, or they have no equity value at all. So if there is no equity value, it is not considered a countable asset.

Chapter 8: VA Benefits

United States veterans may be eligible for a broad range of benefits including long-term care. These benefits are provided by the United States Department of Veterans Affairs and are codified in Title 38 of the United States Code.

Generally, eligibility for VA benefits is based upon discharge from active military service except under dishonorable conditions. Active service means full-time service. Generally it does not include reserve only service, nor any veteran or dependent wanted on an outstanding felony warrant or bad conduct or court marshal. However there are exceptions and you should contact the nearest VSO in your local regional office.

The VA offers many programs. The key is to get your loved one enrolled as soon as possible in the VA system. It takes a long time to work through the system. Don't wait until you NEED the VA. Do it now.

Hospice is also available from the VA. First you have to contact the VA and get a rating (http://www.benefits.va.gov/warms/bookc.asp). A rating is how the VA weighs your loved one's disability and service record. Then the vet will be assigned a primary care physician (PCP). The PCP then can refer him to a geriatric program. Once in the geriatric program, ask for your loved one to be in palliative care. This means your loved one agrees that he does not want anything done to prolong his life or "cure" him. He wants to be kept comfortable and not in pain.

Most benefits require at least one day of service during wartime. These periods are defined according to the following:

Code of Federal Regulations, Title 38, Part 3, 2

Mexican Border May 9, 1916 to April 5, 1917

World War I April 6, 1917 through November 11, 1918/April 1, 1920 if served in Russia

World War II Dec 7 1941 through Dec 31, 1946

Important Note: Those who served in the Merchant Marines (like my father) have been given Veteran Status for WWII service.

Korean War June 27, 1950 through Jan 31 1955

Vietnam War Aug 5, 1964 through May 7 1975/ February 28, 1961 if served in Vietnam

Persian Gulf War Aug 2, 1990 through Nov 11, 1998

Iraq War (dates to be determined)

Afghanistan War (dates to be determined)

To qualify for most veteran's benefits you must have served 90 days and your discharge cannot be dishonorable. You need serve only one day during the wartime period; for example, if you joined November 10, 1998, served one day, and then served 89 days after November 11, 1998 you would qualify for benefits.

You need not have served overseas. You could have been assigned a desk job in the States and never seen a gun and you would still qualify. You do not need to have suffered a service-connected disability. Of course, veterans who do have a service-connected disability get priority. Disability pensions provide benefits for the spouse.

The veteran will need to submit a copy of their **DD214 DD215** or **WD form**—these are copies of your service discharge forms. If you can't find your papers, contact your local American Legion or Veterans Service office.

CHAPTER 8: VA BENEFITS

Form 0845 designates you as the authorized person to discuss the veteran's claims. Do not send anything to the VA without this form designating you as the authorized person in charge of your Veterans Affairs. Even if you are the spouse/dependent and have filed a Power of Attorney, the VA will only recognize Form 845 (http://www.va.gov/vaforms/form_detail.asp?FormNo=21-0845). Keep a copy of this form, otherwise you will get the runaround, as I have mentioned.

Approximately 30 days after you have sent in all your paperwork, call the regional office, not your local VA, and ask them if they have the form 0845 filed on behalf of veteran "John Doe 1234" and include the last four digits of the social security number. If and only if the regional office does not have the form, call the local VA, tell the local VSO that regional does not have the claim form, and ask for the local VA to put a trace on the file. Then call every week to follow up.

My husband was in priority group 8, meaning he served during designated wartime and was discharged with honorable service. He was disabled, but the disability was not service-connected. Many veterans who qualify for benefits do not apply because they erroneously believe the disability must have been incurred during service.

No outside entity is allowed to charge a veteran or their dependent for filing out any VA forms. The local Veterans Office has a Veterans Service Officer (VSO) or staff officer who will assist the veteran or his or her dependent at no charge. In addition, I have personally found the local American Legion post to be extremely useful and helpful in explaining benefits and walking you through the process. All this paperwork is confusing to fill out and the time taken to process a claim without help is unbelievable, ridiculous, and redundant. Some veterans do not apply for benefits because they do not know the benefits exist and/or how to access them. Please get help in filling out the forms. Veterans die while paperwork is being mishandled, which is an outrage.

The VA does provide for nursing home care but it is not well funded. There are millions of veterans who qualify for nursing home care, yet there are only a minuscule number of beds. At present, in order to get into a nursing home, the veteran must have a service-related disability and be at least 60 percent disabled. If you do not have a service-connected disability although you are 80 percent disabled, you will never get in. I believe this is a crime and the federal government needs to properly fund all benefits, which are on the books so that every veteran can qualify for all benefits. The VA also needs to clean up the backlog of claims.

In some cases, veterans may be eligible for community living centers. If you are enrolled in the VA health care system, you may qualify for a CLC. This again depends on funding. It is easier to get into a CLC than a regular VA nursing home. The gatekeeper for this is the VA social worker.

The VA is short on resources. Often there is just not enough funding for different programs and nowhere is this truer than in long-term care. The VA has set up a priority program where veterans qualify for resources but need priority for a higher rating.

The following are the priority groups, as defined by the VA:

Enrollment Priority Groups

Priority Group 1:

- Veterans with VA service-connected disabilities rated 50 percent or more.

- Veterans assigned a total disability rating for compensation based on un-employability.

Priority Group 2:

- Veterans with VA service-connected disabilities rated 30 percent or 40 percent.

Priority Group 3:

- Veterans who are former POWs.

- Veterans awarded the Purple Heart Medal.

- Veterans awarded the Medal of Honor.

- Veterans whose discharge was for a disability incurred or aggravated in the line of duty.

- Veterans with VA service-connected disabilities rated 10 percent or 20 percent.

- Veterans awarded special eligibility classification under Title 38, U.S.C., 1151, "benefits for individuals disabled by treatment or vocational rehabilitation."

Priority Group 4:

- Veterans receiving increased compensation or pension based on their need for regular aid and attendance or by reason of being permanently housebound.

- Veterans determined by VA to be catastrophically disabled.

Priority Group 5:

- Non-service-connected veterans, non-compensable service-connected Veterans rated zero percent, whose annual income and/or net worth are not greater than the VA financial thresholds.

Priority Group 6:

- Compensable zero percent service-connected veterans.

- Veterans exposed to ionizing radiation during atmospheric testing or during the occupation of Hiroshima and Nagasaki.

- Project 112/SHAD participants.

- Veterans who served in the Republic of Vietnam between January 9, 1962 and May 7, 1975.

- Veterans of the Persian Gulf War who served in the Southwest Asia Theater of combat operations between August 2, 1990 and November 11, 1998.

- Veterans who served in a theater of combat operations and discharged from active duty on or after January 28, 2003, for five years post discharge.

Priority Group 7:

- Veterans with incomes below the geographic means test (GMT) income thresholds and who gave to pay the applicable copayment.

Priority Group 8:

Veterans with gross household incomes:

- Above the VA Means Test thresholds who were enrolled as of January 16, 2003 and who agreed to pay the applicable copayment;

Or

- Not exceeding the VA Means Test thresholds or GMT income thresholds by more than 10% and who agree to pay the applicable copayment—effective June 15, 2009.

CHAPTER 8: VA BENEFITS

Other Helpful Tips for Veterans

The following are important pieces of information and advice I'd like to share with you:

- If your loved one is an eligible veteran, is over the age of 65, and served just one day during the period of war, s/he is eligible for benefits.

- If your loved one is permanently and totally disabled, they are eligible.

- For a monthly pension, the maximum amount is $1,949. If the veteran has no dependents, then the maximum amount is $1,644.

- There is an asset limitation. This amount is very subjective, but is usually less than $10,000 in assets. There is no five-year look-back period when assessing VA benefits as there is in applying for Medicaid benefits.

- Always ask about Aide and Attendance. Aide and Attendance is extremely valuable if you keep your loved one at home. A family member can be paid through Aide and Attendance.

- Few attorneys are knowledgeable about VA benefits, so search for one that knows the law and is recommended by others who have gone through this before you.

- There are many service benefit private organizations that (for a fee) will help you fill out the necessary documents. The fee is usually one month's benefits; it is my personal opinion that it is worthwhile to pay this fee. Unfortunately, some (as in any business) have unscrupulous agents whose main purpose is not to get your benefits but to gain access to all your financial information and then sell you insurance products such as annuities and life insurance. The VSO at your local VA office can help you fill out the paperwork. This is a free service but there are huge caseloads and it may be many months before the paperwork is complete and finished.

STATE VETERANS SERVICE: Every state has at least one state veterans' home. These homes are available through your State Veterans Administration. State Veterans Administration is not the same as the Federal Veterans Administration. Admittance to these homes is not dependent on assets or income. There is a charge (usually only a few hundred dollars a month) and every state veterans' home I have visited is really very nice and offers good company. In fact, most of the employees are themselves veterans, which means they have a vested interest in providing your loved one with excellent care.

If your loved one served in the Merchant Marines, there is a beautiful home in Snug Harbor S. C. I toured this facility with my dad. It was on the ocean and looked like a resort. I believe this is the only one in the country, but if you get a chance to place your loved one there, it is a great place.

The Affordable Care Act of 2010 aka "Obamacare"

In my opinion, this Act did not negatively affect benefits for caregivers and their loved ones. As of this writing The Supreme Court of the United States is still determining if the Act is constitutional or not.

Chapter 9: The Importance of Self-Care and Avoiding Burnout

Burnout is very common amongst caregivers and people working in demanding social positions. While nearly everyone experiences physical fatigue, burnout is the emotional equivalent of chronic fatigue. People who are experiencing burnout may continue to work, but they are less effective in their positions because they are detached emotionally for the sake of self-preservation. A sense of strange apathy or hopelessness may start to cloud their experience of a task, profession, or undertaking that previously invigorated them. Signs you may be experiencing burnout include: physical fatigue, a constant feeling of being overwhelmed, feeling you are always a few steps behind, and most notably, a sense of apathy or hopelessness that what you are doing is making a difference.

Burnout is common in caring for aging parents. Not only can caring for an aging parent be physically and mentally taxing, but the many intense emotions that accompany it provide a prime situation for an adult child to become burnt out. It is important to remember that caring for an aging parent can be a decades-long process and that running on fumes for too long will have a disastrous effect on your health and wellbeing. As with many health problems, prevention is the best medicine. Only good self-care will help you maintain your own life and identity.

Burnout is a normal part of life. One would be hard-pressed to find a person who hasn't experienced burnout in either their personal or professional lives. But like many physical and emotional health problems, it is preventable. The only proven way to prevent and treat burnout is to practice excellent self care.

What is Self Care?

Self care is the lifelong practice of protecting and maintaining your emotional, physical, and mental health. Self care is the equivalent of flight attendants encouraging passengers to put on their own oxygen mask before assisting others. We cannot effectively help others until we have taken care of ourselves. There is a false and damaging belief that helping others before you help yourself makes you selfless and more dedicated to those you're serving. But martyrdom is not usually the most effective way to help people. Any mental health worker, doctor, nurse, or other care provider who has had a long and successful career without getting burnt out practices effective self care regularly. Self care is viewed by most mental health professionals as mandatory, and you should consider it as such. Many people's instinct when caring for an aging parent is to forgo self care so that they have more time to care for their parent. But that is detrimental to all parties. If you are caring for an aging parent, a concrete, reliable self-care plan is not optional.

Some self-care practices include: exercise, nutrition, good sleep hygiene, adequate social time, meditation, talk therapy, art and other hobbies, or any other practice that promotes health and well-being. Self care often manifests in small acts such as treating yourself to a great cup of coffee or a peaceful walk through your neighborhood. Sometimes a nice glass of wine or some retail therapy can be effective self-care, but generally activities that involve substance use or acquiring material goods do not have longevity as effective and healthy forms of self-care.

Self-care needs change throughout the life cycle and as your emotional landscape changes over months and years. What worked a few years ago may not work now. If you are unsure of what your self-care plan looks like now, it is critical to establish a regular practice. Experiment with different activities: take a yoga class, go for a hike, call up an old friend to talk, get a pedicure, try aromatherapy, or give your closet a good cleaning. Eventually you will find something that leaves you feeling refreshed and calm and as though you have honored yourself. The only thing not usually recommended, other than using alcohol, drugs, gambling, or other risky behaviors, is making your self-care about others. While volunteering at a soup kitchen or watching your neighbor's children for a few hours may make you feel good, it is ultimately energy and time spent on others. Your self care needs to be solely about you. With all the time and energy you are spending taking care of your parent, as well as other relationships in your life, you deserve to have a little time every week reserved for just you. So take it. No one else is going to give it to you.

Chapter 10: Parting Words

So, as you can see, the saying "GROW OLD WITH ME; THE BEST IS YET TO BE" is a lie. I hate to say it, but anyone who is currently struggling through end-of-life care with a loved one knows this is not the best time. It is a devastatingly difficult time. I only hope to ease your pain as much as I can by offering you some direction that may save you some frustration at a time when agony and heartache are already overwhelmingly present.

This is a poem by Darnell Owen. He cared for his wife who was stricken with Alzheimer's. It has been published in countless books, websites, and other resources for caregivers. This is what kept me going. I hope it brings some sense of peace to you as well.

Don't try to make me understand.
Let me rest and know you're with me.
Kiss my cheek and hold my hand.
I'm confused beyond your concept.
I am sad and sick and lost.
All I know is that I need you
To be with me at all cost.

Do not lose your patience with me.
Do not scold or curse or cry.
I can't help the way I'm acting.
Can't be different 'though I try.
Just remember that I need you,
That the best of me is gone.
Please don't fail to stand beside me,
Love me 'til my life is done.

- Owen Darnell (1921-2005)

Chapter 10: Parting Words

I hope this guide has been of help to you. I welcome your feedback at <u>DrIreneRodway@gmail.com</u>. If this book has been of value to you I would appreciate it if you would give it a review on Amazon.com.

Glossary of Terms

(From the US Department of Health & Human Services Website: http://longtermcare.gov/the-basics/glossary/)

Accelerated Death Benefit

A life insurance policy feature that lets you use some of the policy's death benefit prior to death.

Activities of Daily Living (ADLs)

Basic actions that independently functioning individuals perform on a daily basis:

- Bathing
- Dressing
- Transferring (moving to and from a bed or a chair)
- Eating
- Caring for incontinence

Many public programs determine eligibility for services according to a person's need for help with ADLs. Many long-term care insurance policies use the inability to do a certain number of ADLs (such as 2 of 6) as criteria for paying benefits.

Acute Care

Recovery is the primary goal of acute care. Physician, nurse, or other skilled professional services are typically required and usually provided in a doctor's office or hospital. Acute care is usually short term.

Adult Day Services

Services provided during the day at a community-based center. Programs address the individual needs of functionally or cognitively impaired adults. These structured, comprehensive programs provide social and support services in a protective setting during any part of a day, but not 24-hour care. Many adult day service programs include health-related services.

Adult Day Services

Services provided during the day at a community-based center. Programs address the individual needs of functionally or cognitively impaired adults. These structured, comprehensive programs provide social and support services in a protective setting during any part of a day, but not 24-hour care. Many adult day service programs include health-related services.

Advanced Directive

(also called Health Care Directive, Advanced Health Care Directive, or Living Will) Legal document that specifies whether you would like to be kept on artificial life support if you become permanently unconscious or are otherwise dying and unable to speak for yourself. It also specifies other aspects of health care you would like under those circumstances.

Aging and Disability Resource Centers (ADRCs)

ADRCs serve as single points of entry into the long-term supports and services system for older adults and people with disabilities. Through integration or coordination of existing aging and disability service systems, ADRC programs raise visibility about the full range of options that are available, provide objective information, advice, counseling and assistance, empower people to make informed decisions about their long-term supports, and help people more easily access public and private long-term supports and services programs.

Alzheimer's Disease

Progressive, degenerative form of dementia that causes severe intellectual deterioration. First symptoms are impaired memory, followed by impaired thought and speech, and finally complete helplessness.

Annuity

A contract in which an individual gives an insurance company money that is later distributed back to the person over time. Annuity contracts traditionally provide a guaranteed distribution of income over time, until the death of the person or persons named in the contract or until a final date, whichever comes first.

Arthritis

Disease involving inflammation of a joint or joints in the body.

Assisted Living Facility

Residential living arrangement that provides individualized personal care, assistance with Activities of Daily Living, help with medications, and services such as laundry and housekeeping. Facilities may also provide health and medical care, but care is not as intensive as care offered at a nursing home. Types and sizes of facilities vary, ranging from small homes to large apartment-style complexes. Levels of care and services also vary. Assisted living facilities allow people to remain relatively independent.

Bathing

Washing oneself by sponge bath or in the bathtub or shower. One of the six Activities of Daily Living (ADLs)

Benefit Triggers (Triggers)

Insurance companies use benefit triggers as criteria to determine when you are eligible to receive benefits. The most common benefit triggers for long-term care insurance are:

1. Needing help with two or more Activities of Daily Living

2. Having a Cognitive Impairment such as Alzheimer's Disease

Benefits

Monetary sum paid by an insurance company to a recipient or to a care provider for services that the insurance policy covers.

Board and Care Home

(also called Group Home) Residential private homes designed to provide housing, meals, housekeeping, personal care services, and supports to frail or disabled residents. At least one caregiver is on the premises at all times. In many states, Board and Care Homes are licensed or certified and must meet criteria for facility safety, types of services provided, and the number and type of residents they can care for. Board and Care Homes are often owned and managed by an individual or family involved in their everyday operation.

Caregiver

A caregiver is anyone who helps care for an elderly individual or person with a disability who lives at home. Caregivers usually provide assistance with activities of daily living and other essential activities like shopping, meal preparation, and housework.

Charitable Remainder Trust

Special tax-exempt irrevocable trust written to comply with federal tax laws and regulations. You transfer cash or assets into the trust and may receive some income from it for life or a specified number of years (not to exceed 20). The minimum payout rate is 5 percent and the maximum is 50 percent. At your death, the remaining amount in the trust goes to the charity that you designated as part of the trust arrangement.

Chronically Ill

Having a long-lasting or recurrent illness or condition that causes you to need help with Activities of Daily Living and often other health and support services. The condition is expected to last for at least 90 consecutive days. The term used in tax-qualified long-term care insurance policies to describe a person who needs long-term care because of an inability to do a certain number of Activities of Daily Living without help, or because of a severe cognitive impairment such as Alzheimer's Disease.

Cognitive Impairment

Deficiency in short or long-term memory, orientation to person, place and time, deductive or abstract reasoning, or judgment as it relates to safety awareness. Alzheimer's Disease is an example of a cognitive impairment.

Community Spouse

Spouse of a nursing home resident applying for or receiving Medicaid long-term care services.

Community-Based Services

Services and service settings in the community, such as adult day services, home delivered meals, or transportation services. Often referred to as home- and community-based services, they are designed to help older people and people with disabilities stay in their homes as independently as possible.

Continence

Ability to maintain control of bowel and bladder functions, or when unable to maintain control of these functions, the ability to perform associated personal hygiene such as caring for a catheter or colostomy bag. This is one of the six Activities of Daily Living.

Continuing Care Retirement Communities (CCRC)

Retirement complex that offers a range of services and levels of care. Residents may move first into an independent living unit, a private apartment, or a house on the campus. The CCRC provides social and housing-related services and often also has an assisted living unit and an on-site or affiliated nursing home. If and when residents can no longer live independently in their apartment or home, they move into assisted living or the CCRC's nursing home.

Countable Assets

Assets whose value is counted in determining financial eligibility for Medicaid. They include:

- Vehicles other than the one used primarily for transportation

- Life insurance with a face value over $1,500

- Bank accounts and trusts

Your home provided that your spouse or child does not live there and its equity value is greater than $500,000 ($750,000 in some states)

CPR (Cardiopulmonary Resuscitation)

Combination of rescue breathing (mouth-to-mouth resuscitation) and chest compressions used if someone isn't breathing or circulating blood adequately. CPR can restore circulation of oxygen-rich blood to the brain.

Custodial Care

(also called personal care) Non-skilled service or care, such as help with bathing, dressing, eating, getting in and out of bed or chair, moving around, and using the bathroom.

Dementia

Deterioration of mental faculties due to a disorder of the brain.

Disabled

For Medicaid eligibility purposes, a disabled person is someone whose physical or mental condition prevents him or her from doing enough work or the type of work needed for self-support. The condition must be expected to last for at least a year or be expected to result in death. Persons receiving disability benefits through Supplemental Security Income (SSI), Social Security, or Medicare automatically meet this criterion.

Do Not Resuscitate Order (DNR)

Written order from a doctor that resuscitation should not be attempted if a person suffers cardiac or respiratory arrest. A DNR order may be instituted on the basis of an Advance Directive from a person, or from someone entitled to make decisions on the person's behalf, such as a health care proxy. In some jurisdictions, such orders can also be instituted on the basis of a physician's own initiative, usually when resuscitation would not alter the ultimate outcome of a disease. Any person who does not wish to undergo lifesaving treatment in the event of cardiac or respiratory arrest can get a DNR order, although

DNR orders are more common when a person with a fatal illness wishes to die without painful or invasive medical procedures.

Dressing

Putting on and taking off all items of clothing and any necessary braces, fasteners, or artificial limbs. This is one of the six Activities of Daily Living.

Durable Power of Attorney

Legal document that gives someone else the authority to act on your behalf on matters that you specify. The power can be specific to a certain task or broad to cover many financial duties. You can specify if you want the power to start immediately or upon mental incapacity. For the document to be valid, you must sign it before you become disabled.

Eating

Feeding oneself by getting food into the body from a receptacle or by a feeding tube or intravenously. It is one of the six Activities of Daily Living.

Elimination Period

(also known as a Deductible Period or Benefit Waiting Period) Specified amount of time at the beginning of a disability during which you receive covered services, but the policy does not pay benefits. A Service Day Deductible Period is satisfied by each day of the period on which you receive covered services. A Calendar Day or Disability Day Deductible Period doesn't require that you receive covered services during the entire deductible period, but only requires that you meet the policy's benefit triggers during that time period.

Equity Value

Fair market value of property minus any liabilities on the property such as mortgages or loans.

Estate Recovery

Process by which Medicaid recovers an amount of money from the estate of a person who received Medicaid. The amount Medicaid recovers cannot be greater than the amount it contributed to the person's medical care.

Exempt Assets

(also called Non-countable Assets) Assets whose value is not counted in determining financial eligibility for Medicaid. They include:

- Personal belongings

- One vehicle

- Life insurance with a face value under $1,500

- Your home provided that your spouse or child lives there and its equity value is less than $500,000 ($750,000 in some states)

Federal Poverty Level

Income standard that the federal government issues annually which reflects increases in prices, measured by the Consumer Price Index.

Financial Eligibility

Assessment of a person's available income and assets to determine if he or she meets Medicaid eligibility requirements.

Functional Eligibility

Assessment of a person's care needs to determine if he or she meets Medicaid eligibility requirements for payment of long-term care services. The assessment may include a person's ability to perform Activities of Daily Living or the need for skilled care.

General Medicaid Eligibility Requirements

You must be:

- A resident of the state in which you are applying
- Either a United States citizen or a legally admitted alien
- Age 65 or over, or
- Meet Medicaid's rules for disability, or blind

Group Home

(also called Board and Care Home) Residential private homes designed to provide housing, meals, housekeeping, personal care services, and supports to frail or disabled residents. At least one caregiver is onsite at all times. In many states, group homes are licensed or certified and must meet criteria for facility safety, types of services provided, and the number and type of residents they can care for. Group homes are often owned and managed by an individual or family involved in their everyday operation.

Health Care Proxy

Legal document in which you name someone to make health care decisions for you if, for any reason and at any time, you become unable to make or communicate those decisions for yourself.

High Blood Pressure

Blood pressure is the force of blood pushing against your blood vessel walls. High blood pressure is when that force, as measured by a blood pressure cuff, is elevated above normal limits.

Homemaker

Licensed Homemaker Services provides "hands-off" care such as helping with cooking and running errands. Often referred to as "Personal Care Assistants" or "Companions." This is the rate charged by a non-Medicare-certified, licensed agency.

Homemaker or Chore Services

Help with general household activities such as meal preparation, routine household care, and heavy household chores such as washing floors or windows or shoveling snow.

Hospice Care

Short-term, supportive care for individuals who are terminally ill (have a life expectancy of six months or less). Hospice care focuses on pain management and emotional, physical, and spiritual support for the patient and family. It can be provided at home or in a hospital, nursing home, or hospice facility. Medicare typically pays for hospice care. Hospice care is not usually considered long-term care.

Incontinence

Inability to maintain control of bowel and bladder functions as well as the inability to perform associated personal hygiene such as caring for a catheter or colostomy bag. Continence is one of the six Activities of Daily Living.

Informal Caregiver

Any person who provides long-term care services without pay.

Instrumental Activities of Daily Living

Activities that are not necessary for basic functioning, but are necessary in order to live independently. These activities may include:

- Doing light housework
- Preparing and cleaning up after meals
- Taking medication
- Shopping for groceries or clothes
- Using the telephone
- Managing money
- Taking care of pets
- Using communication devices
- Getting around the community
- Responding to emergency alerts such as fire alarms

Living Will

(also called Health Care Directive or Advanced Health Care Directive) Legal document that specifies whether you would like to be kept on artificial life support if you become permanently unconscious or are otherwise dying and unable to speak for yourself. It also specifies other aspects of health care you would like under those circumstances.

Long-Term Care

Services and supports necessary to meet health or personal care needs over an extended period of time.

Long-Term Care Facility

(also called Long Nursing Home or Convalescent Care Facility) Licensed facility that provides general nursing care to those who are chronically ill or unable to take care of daily living needs.

Long-Term Care Insurance

Insurance policy designed to offer financial support to pay for long-term care services.

Long-Term Care Services

Services that include medical and non-medical care for people with a chronic illness or disability. Long-term care helps meet health or personal needs. Most long-term care services assists people with Activities of Daily Living, such as dressing, bathing, and using the bathroom. Long-term care can be provided at home, in the community, or in a facility. For purposes of Medicaid eligibility and payment, long-term care services are those provided to an individual who requires a level of care equivalent to that received in a nursing facility.

Look-Back Period

Five-year period prior to a person's application for Medicaid payment of long-term care services. The Medicaid agency determines if any transfers of assets have taken place during that period that would disqualify the applicant from receiving Medicaid benefits for a period of time called the penalty period.

Medicaid

Joint federal and state public assistance program for financing health care for low-income people. It pays for health care services for those with low incomes or very high medical bills relative to income and assets. It is the largest public payer of long-term care services.

Medical Power of Attorney

Legal document that allows you to name someone to make health care decisions for you if, for any reason and at any time, you become unable to make or communicate those decisions for yourself.

Medicare

Federal program that provides hospital and medical expense benefits for people over age 65, or those meeting specific disability standards. Benefits for nursing home and home health services are limited.

Medicare Supplement Insurance

(also called Medigap Coverage) Private insurance policy that covers gaps in Medicare coverage.

Medigap Insurance

(also called Medicare Supplement Insurance) Private insurance policy that covers gaps in Medicare coverage.

National Association of Insurance Commissioners (NAIC)

Membership organization of state insurance commissioners. One of its goals is to promote uniformity of state regulation and legislation related to insurance.

Non-countable Assets

(also called Exempt Assets) Assets whose value is not counted in determining financial eligibility for Medicaid. They include:

- Personal belongings

- One vehicle

- Life insurance with a face value under $1,500

- Your home provided that your spouse or child lives there and its equity value is less than $500,000 ($750,000 in some states)

Nursing Home

(also called Long-Term Care Facility or Convalescent Care Facility) Licensed facility that provides general nursing care to those who are chronically ill or unable to take care of daily living needs.

Osteoporosis

Bone disease characterized by a reduction in bone density. Bones become porous and brittle as a result of calcium loss. People with osteoporosis are more vulnerable to breaking bones.

Partnership Long-Term Care Insurance Policy

Private long-term care insurance policy that allows you to keep some or all of your assets if you apply for Medicaid after using up your policy's benefits. The Deficit Reduction Act of 2005 allows any state to establish a Partnership Program. Under a Partnership policy, the amount of Medicaid spend-down protection you receive is generally equal to the amount of benefits you received under your private Partnership policy. (State-specific program designs vary.)

Personal Care

(also called custodial care) Non-skilled service or care, such as help with bathing, dressing, eating, getting in and out of bed or chair, moving around, and using the bathroom.

Respite Care

Temporary care which is intended to provide time off for those who care for someone on a regular basis. Respite care is typically 14 to 21 days of care per year and can be provided in a nursing home, adult day service center, or at home by a private party.

Reverse Mortgage

Type of loan based on home equity that enables older homeowners (age 62 or older) to convert part of their equity in their homes into tax-free income without having to sell the home, give up title, or take on a new monthly mortgage payment. Instead of making monthly payments to a lender, as you do with a regular mortgage, a lender makes payments to you. The loan, along with financing costs and interest on the loan, does not need to be repaid until the homeowner dies or no longer lives in the home.

Skilled Care

Nursing care such as help with medications and caring for wounds, and therapies such as occupational, speech, respiratory, and physical therapy. Skilled care usually requires the services of a licensed professional such as a nurse, doctor, or therapist.

Skilled Care Needs

Services requiring the supervision and care of a nurse or physician, such as assistance with oxygen, maintenance of a feeding tube, or frequent injections.

Spend Down

Requirement that an individual spend most of his or her income and assets to pay for care before he or she can satisfy Medicaid's financial eligibility criteria.

Supervisory Care

Long-term care service for people with memory or orientation problems. Supervision ensures that people don't harm themselves or others because their memory, reasoning, and orientation to person, place, or time are impaired.

Supplemental Security Income (SSI)

Program administered by the Social Security Administration that provides financial assistance to needy persons who are disabled or aged 65 or older. Many states provide Medicaid without further application to persons who are eligible for SSI.

Transfer of Assets

Giving away property for less than it is worth or for the sole purpose of becoming eligible for Medicaid. Transferring assets during the look-back period results in disqualification for Medicaid payment of long-term care services for a penalty period.

Transferring

Moving into and out of a bed, chair, or wheelchair. Transferring is one of the six Activities of Daily Living.

Suggested Reading

For more information and in-depth coverage of specific topics raised in this book, see also:

How to Care for Aging Parents by Virginia Morris

This book is an in-depth exploration of the topic. It has long been regarded as an authority on the subject, and has been updated several times to keep information fresh and current.

The Complete Eldercare Planner by Joy Loverde

This lengthy book is chock-full of useful charts, graphs, and worksheets to help you along your journey. Focuses more on emotions and housing than financial issues.

Dementia resources:

An Unintended Journey by Janet Yoga Shagam

Shagam outlines the process, both practical and emotional, of the task of caring for a parent with dementia that is experienced by the children of over five million dementia patients in the US. As the author has both medical training on the topic and personal experience, Shagam's book is one of the top titles in the country on the subject of dementia.

Complaints of a Dutiful Daughter (film) dir. Deborah Hoffman

Deborah Hoffman chronicles the emotional roller coaster that accompanied caring for her mother, who suffered from dementia, in her final years. Touching and honest, this film is a must-see for anyone caring for elderly dementia patients.

For elders facing their own death:

Staring at the Sun by Irvin D. Yalom

Philospher and respected psychologist Irvin Yalom wrote this book to address people's fear of death and dying. Many who read it feel it is a transformative experience and allows them to enjoy the rest of their lives more fully.

Facing Death by Christine Longaker

After her husband's death at the age of 24, Longaker devoted her life to the study and care of the suffering of people nearing death. This book maps out the four major tasks of those living and dying and offers hope to those who have a shorter road ahead of them.

References

Dychtwalkd, K. (n.d.). *The Aging of America: Triumph or Tragedy?* (VIDEO). Retrieved July 30, 2015, from http://www.huffingtonpost.com/ken-dychtwald/the-aging-of-america-triu_b_613223.html

Centers for Disease Control and Prevention. *Chronic Disease Overview.* (2015, May 18). Retrieved July 31, 2015. http://www.cdc.gov/chronicdisease/overview/

US Department of Health and Human Services *Glossary* (n.d.). Retrieved August 3, 2015, from http://longtermcare.gov/the-basics/glossary/

Administration on Aging (2004). *National Family Caregiver Support Program (FCSP) Complete Resource Guide.* Washington, D.C.: Author.

The National Alliance for Caregiving and AARP (2009*), Caregiving in the U.S. National Alliance for Caregiving. Washington, DC.*

Darnell, Owen. *A Room without Doors* Ormond Beach, FL: Flagler Chapter Alzheimer's Association, 1995

Product Recommendation

I highly recommend the **Medical Health Data Service Medical History Bracelet**. The MHDS system enables hospitals, physicians, nurses and other authorized users, to share a patient's medical history, providing efficiency and reducing the risk of human error in every patient care event. The Director of this company, Dr. William Mason is a personal friend. His mission is to help save lives with this invention that puts your entire medical history and contact information on a USB drive that then can be easily accessed by EMTs, doctors, and hospitals. Find out more here: www.mhds.info

Made in United States
North Haven, CT
08 March 2024